ROSE SECOND OUROBORO

Other NYQ Books by Richard Kostelanetz

Ouroboros (2014)
Recircuits (2009)
Three Poems (2011)

Works of Poetry by Richard Kostelanetz in Other Media

Echo (Silkscreened paper, 1975)
Word Prints (Silkscreened paper, 1976)
Milestones in a Life (Poster, Pittsburgh Poetry on the Buses, 1980)
Antitheses (Hologram, 1985)
Stringtwo (Inkjet print 200' long, 2004)
Warm/Cold (Acetate print, 2004)
Reimagining Rockaway Postcards (Paper prints, 2004)
The East Village (Paper prints, 2004)
Black Writings (Inkjet prints, 2010)
Shorter Ouroboros (Jars, 2011)
Art (Acetate print, 2013)

SECONDOUROBOROS

Richard Kostelanetz

The New York Quarterly Foundation, Inc.
Beacon, New York

NYQ Books™ is an imprint of The New York Quarterly Foundation, Inc.

The New York Quarterly Foundation, Inc.
P. O. Box 470
Beacon, NY 12508

www.nyq.org

Copyright © 2020 by Richard Kostelanetz

All rights reserved. No part of this book may be used or reproduced in any manner whatsoever without written permission of the author except in the case of brief quotations embodied in critical articles and reviews.

First Edition

Set in Minion Pro

Layout and Design by Andrew Morinelli

Library of Congress Control Number: 2020933902

ISBN: 978-1-63045-075-5

For my poetry's publisher,
Ray Hammond

Preface

From the beginning of my work in visual poetry fifty years ago, I wanted to create from words alone images so strong that they would stick in viewers' heads long after their eyes turned away from my works. When I first heard the epithet Afterimage as an honorific among visual artists, I recognized it as analogous to the strongest lines in strictly verbal poetry.

Now that I've seen others claim the epithet Visual Poetry for words embedded in other kinds of images, I feel more reason to declare and extend my original ambition to make the most powerful afterimages available to me with words alone.

Secondouroboros represents a sequel to an earlier collection *Ouroboros* with different visual forms also published by NYQ Books (2014).

Many *Shorter Ouroboros,* all with less than seven letters, I've put into clear circular cylinders, thus making small Sculptures that must be held and spun in a viewer's hand to be "read."

—Richard Kostelanetz, 14 March 2020

ABUTMENTABUTMENTABUTMENTABUTMENT

ACRONYMACRONYMACRONYM

ADDENDUMADDENDUMADDENDUM

ACADEMICACADEMICACADEMICACADEMIC

ACHIEVEACHIEVEACHIEVEACHIEVE

6

ADAMANTADAMANTADAMANTADAMANT

8

ADMINISTERADMINISTERADMINISTER

AGAINSTAGAINSTAGAINSTAGAINSTAGAINST

MENTAILMENTAILMENTAILMENTAILMENTAIL

11

AILANTHUSAILANTHUSAILANTHUSAILANTHUS

ALTERNATIVEALTERNATIVEALTERNATIVE

14

AMELIORATEAMELIORATEAMELIORATE

AMPITHEATERAMPITHEATERAMPITHEATERAMPITHEATER

17

AMPUTATEAMPUTATEAMPUTATEAMPUTATE

ANTINUCLEARANTINUCLEARANTINUCLEAR

ANTIPATHETICANTIPATHETICANTIPATHETIC

19

APARTMENTAPARTMENTAPARTMENT

APERTUREAPERTUREAPERTUREAPERTURE

ARTICLEARTICLEARTICLEARTICLE

ARRANGEMENTARRANGEMENTARRANGEMENT

ARTIFACTARTIFACTARTIFACTARTIFACT

ASPIRINGASPIRINGASPIRINGASPIRING

STRINGENTASTRINGENTASTRINGENTASTRINGENTA

ASTROLABEASTROLABEASTROLABEASTROLABE

ATMOSPHEREATMOSPHEREATMOSPHEREATMOSPHERE

AUTOCRATAUTOCRATAUTOCRATAUTOCRAT

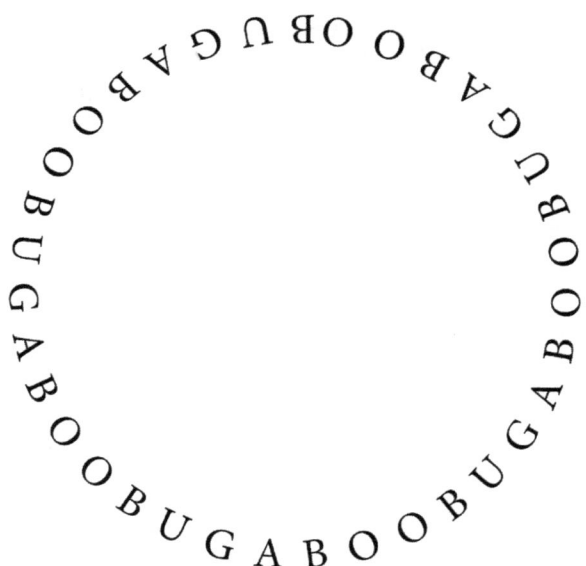

COLLUDECOLLUDECOLLUDECOLLUDE

CUMULUSCUMULUSCUMULUSCUMULUS

DERANGEDERANGEDERANGED

DESCRIBEDESCRIBEDESCRIBE

DIPLOMADIPLOMADIPLOMADIPLOMA

EARLIESTEARLIESTEARLIESTEARLIES (arranged in a circle)

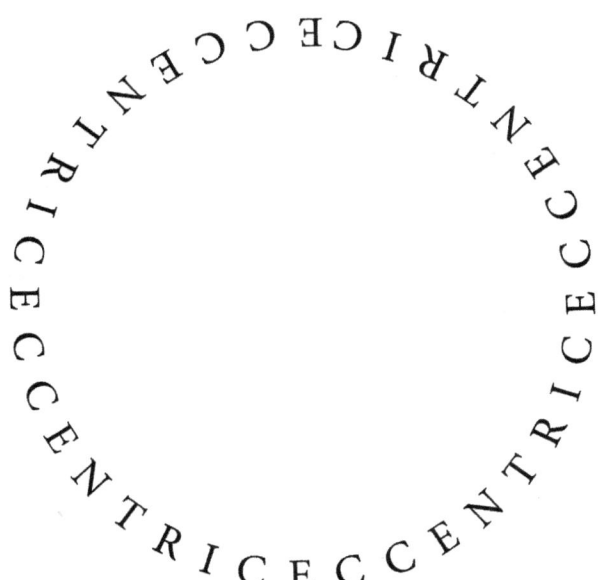

40

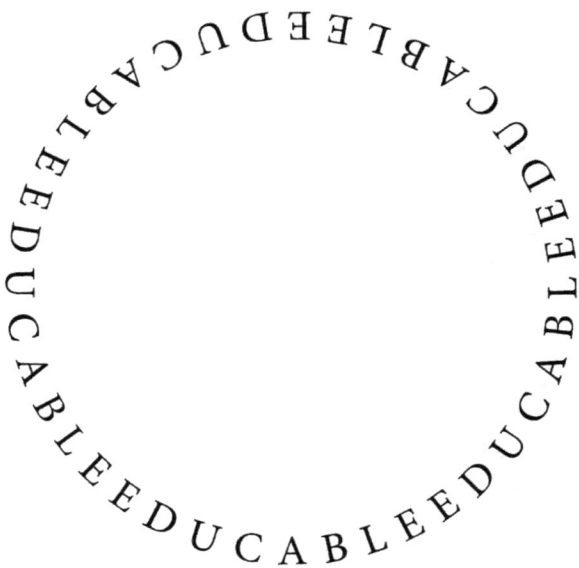

ELABORATEELABORATEELABORATE

ENDANGERENDANGERENDANGERENDANGERENDANGER

ENGAGEMENTENGAGEMENTENGAGEMENT

46

EPIDEMICEPIDEMICEPIDEMICEPIDEMIC

EPHEMERALEPHEMERALEPHEMERALEPHEM (arranged in a circle)

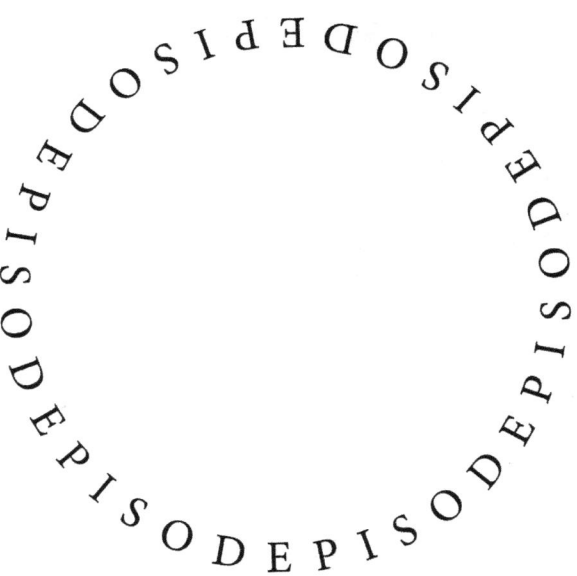

ERSTWHILEERSTWHILEERSTWHILE

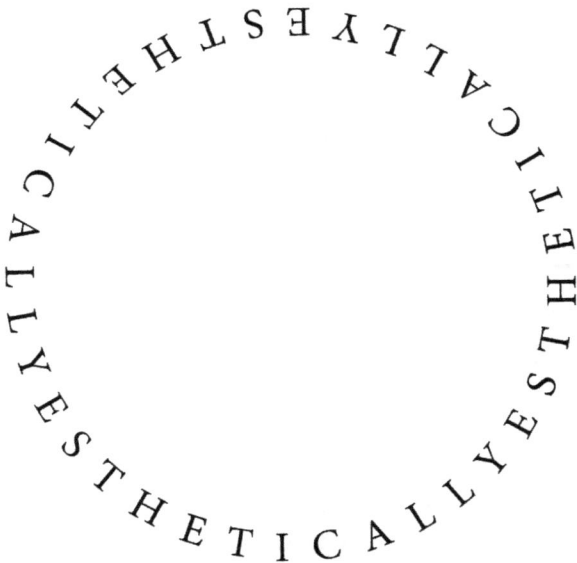

ESTUARYESTUARYESTUARYESTUARY

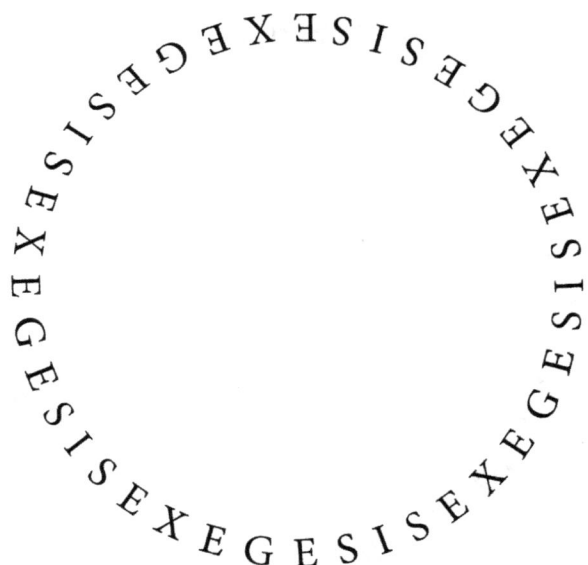

EXTENSIONEXTENSIONEXTENSION

EXTRICATEEXTRICATEEXTRICATEEXTRICATE

HALLELUJAHSHALLELUJAHSH

60

62

IDENTICALIDENTICALIDENTICALIDENTICAL

IMPEACHIMPEACHIMPEACHIMPEACH

IMPERIALIMPERIALIMPERIAL

IMPOSTORIMPOSTORIMPOSTORIMPOSTOR

INCESTUOUSINCESTUOUSINCESTUOUS

INSIDIOUSINSIDIOUSINSIDIOUSINSIDIOUS

INSIPIDINSIPIDINSIPIDINSIPIDINSIPID

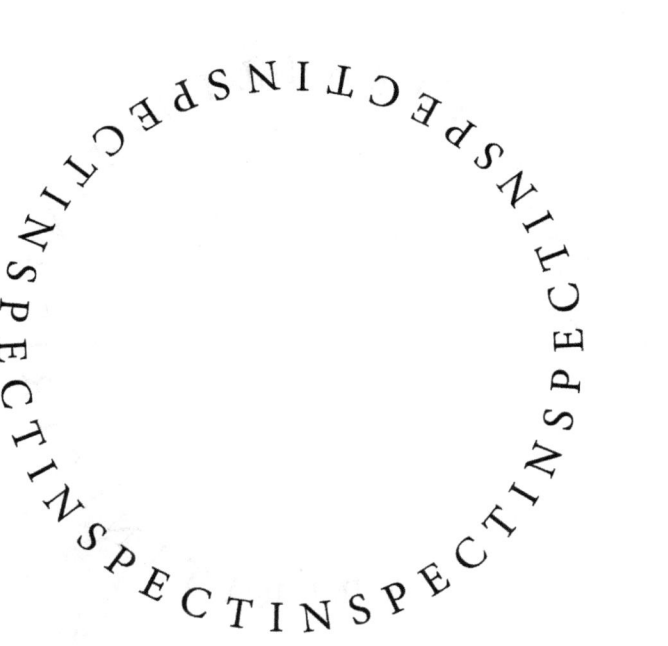

SPIRITINSPIRITINSPIRITINSPIRITINSPIRIT

INSURGENTINSURGENTINSURGENT

INTERESTINTERESTINTERESTINTEREST

INTERVIEWINTERVIEWINTERVIEW

INVOLVEINVOLVEINVOLVE

MUSISTHMUSISTHMUSISTHMUSISTHM

LANGUOROUSLANGUOROUSLANGUOROUS

LOGISTICSLOGISTICSLOGISTICSLOGISTICS

80

MARRIAGEMARRIAGEMARRIAGE

MARTYRDOMARTYRDOMARTYRDOMARTYRDOM

CREMEDIOCREMEDIOCREMEDIO

MEMENTOMEMENTOMEMENTO

METRONOMETRONOMETRONOMETRONOMETRONOMETRONO

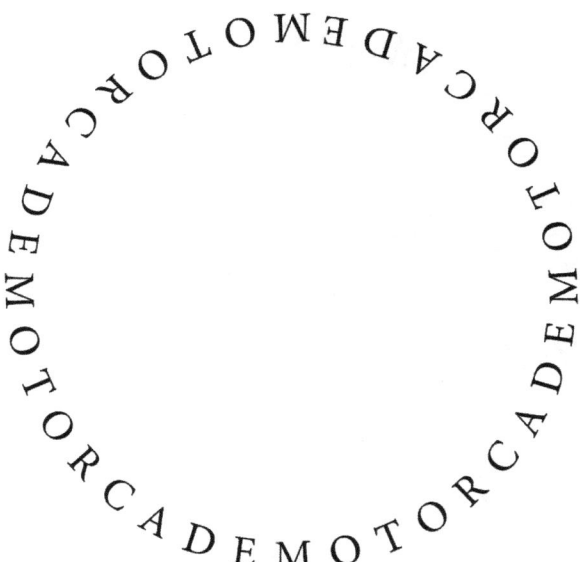

OPINIONOPINIONOPINIONOPINIONOPINION

OUTDOORSOUTDOORSOUTDOORSOUTDOORS

OUTLANDISHOUTLANDISHOUTLANDISHOUTLANDISH

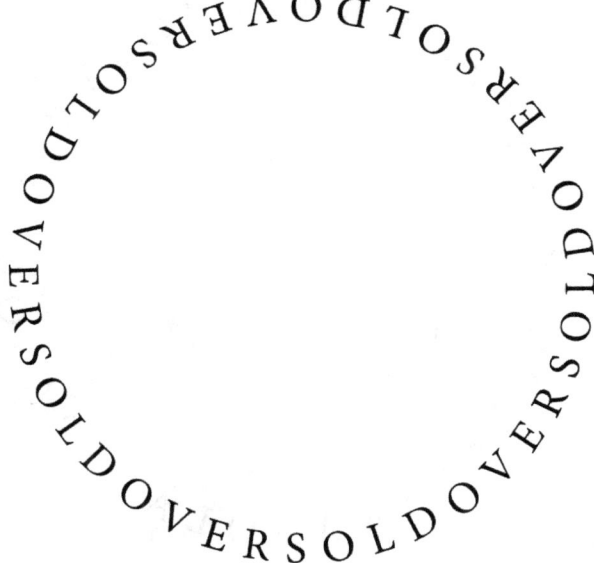

PARAPETSPARAPETSPARAPETSPARAPETS

PIZZICATOPIZZICATOPIZZICATOPIZZICATOPIZZICATO

PRODIGYPRODIGYPRODIGY

99

RAMPANTRAMPANTRAMPANTRAMPANT

100

SIGNATURESIGNATURE

STALEMATESTALEMATESTALEMATESTALEMATE

STEADFASTEADFASTEADFASTEADFASTEADFASTEADFAS

STEREOTYPESTEREOTYPESTEREOTYPE

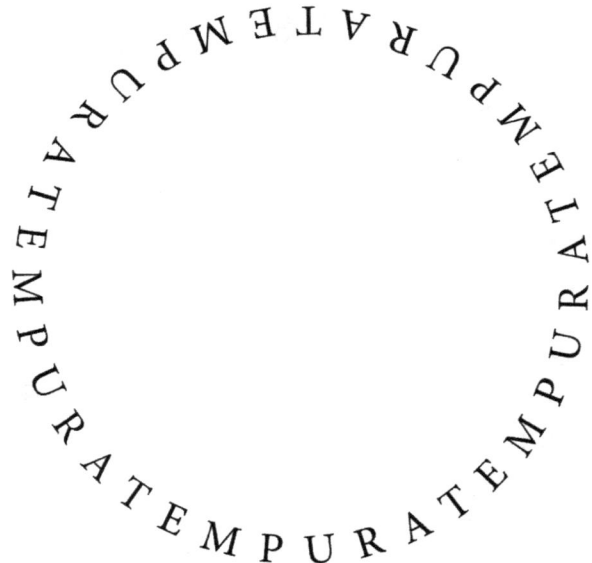

TEENAGETEENAGETEENAGETEENAGE

TESTAMEN(T)TESTAMEN(T)TESTAMEN(T)TESTAMEN(T)

THEORBOTHEORBOTHEORBOTHEORBO

TORNADOTORNADOTORNADOTORNADO

TRANSCRIPTRANSCRIPTRANSCRIPT

111

TRANSPARENTRANSPARENTRANSPARENT (arranged in a circle)

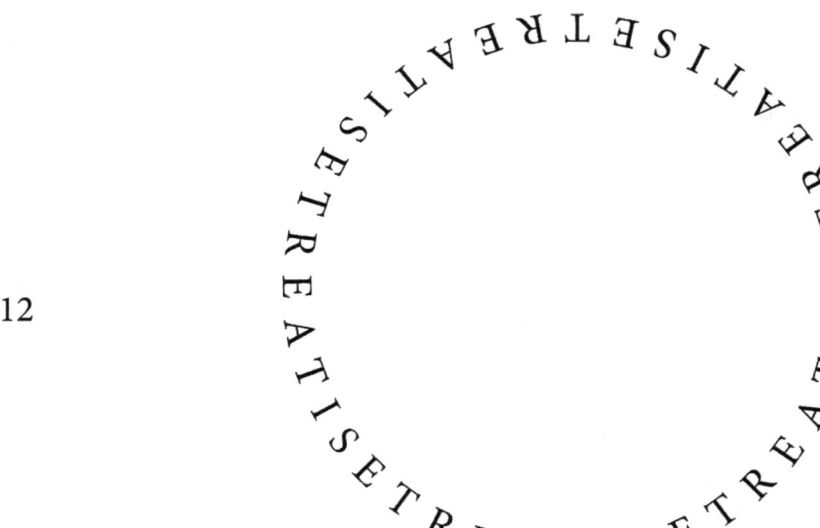

TRUNDLETRUNDLETRUNDLETRUNDLETRUNDLE

TURNABOUTURNABOUTURNABOUTURNABOUT

HUMPTEENTHUMPTEENTHUMPTEENTHUMPTEENTH

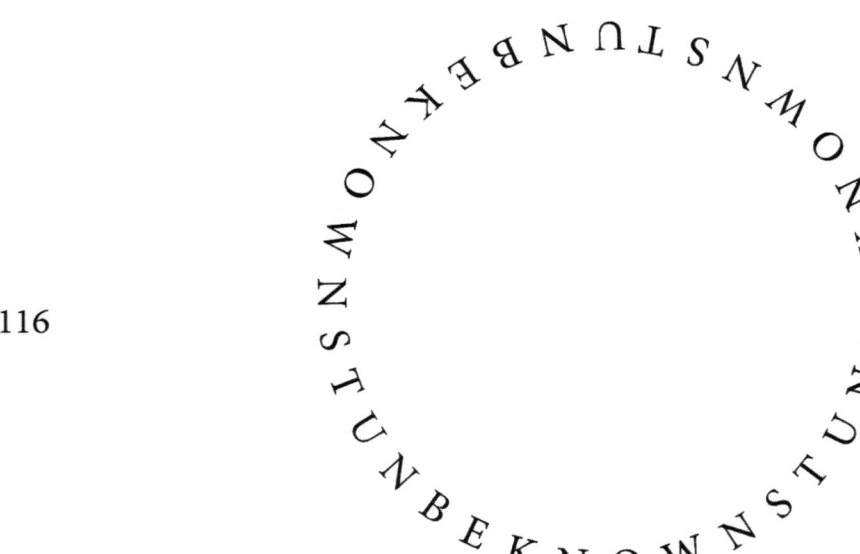

117

BELIEFUNBELIEFUNBELIEFUNBELIEFUNBELIEF

UNDERDOGUNDERDOGUNDERDOGUNDERDOG

UNDERNEATHUNDERNEATH

UNDOINGUNDOINGUNDOING

UNENDINGUNENDINGUNENDINGUNENDING

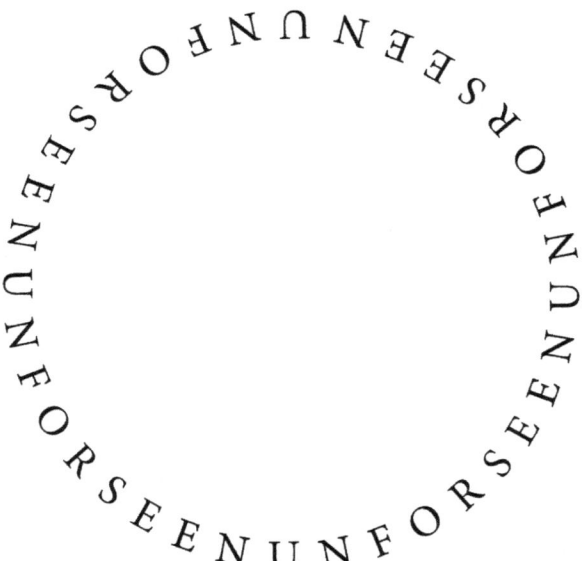

VANILLAVANILLAVANILLAVANILLA

VENTUREVENTUREVENTUREVENTURE

VERANDAVERANDAVERANDAVERANDA

www.ingramcontent.com/pod-product-compliance
Lightning Source LLC
Chambersburg PA
CBHW081328190426
43193CB00044B/2893